FROM NOVICE TO EXECUTIVE: THE PATH TO A SUCCESSFUL CAREER

CONTENT

Introduction
Author's introduction and work experience
Part I: Starting in the Work World
   Chapter 1: Entering the organization
      The power of first impressions
      Understand the corporate culture
   Chapter 2: Developing technical skills
      Continuous learning
      Knowledge renewal
Part II: Interpersonal Relationships
   Chapter 3: Connecting through communication
      Effective communication
      Building strong relationships in the workplace
   Chapter 4: Relationship with superiors
      Strategies to earn the trust of your superiors
      Professionalism and ethics as a subordinate
Part III: Moving up the corporate ladder
   Chapter 5: Asking for promotions and advancements
      Don't directly ask for promotions or advancements
      Identify opportunities
      Let your preparations be known
   Chapter 6: Becoming a leader
      Don't miss opportunities
      Developing leadership skills
      Leading teams effectively
Part IV: Final advice for professional success
   Chapter 7: Developing emotional intelligence
      Definition of emotional intelligence
      The importance of emotional self-regulation
      Managing stress and work pressures
      Developing emotional resilience
Conclusion

INTRODUCTION

From the moment we begin our professional journey, we face a world full of demands and challenges that can feel overwhelming. Successfully navigating this environment requires specific strategies and tools, and in these pages, I will share the ones that have helped me throughout my career so that you too can apply them. This book will provide you with a set of resources, whether you're looking for your first job, seeking to improve your performance, or aiming to climb the organizational ladder.

The goal of this book is to empower you not only with practical advice but also with the mental and emotional tools you need to thrive in a constantly changing work environment. We will explore how to make a memorable first impression, how to build strong relationships, and how to adapt to organizational culture, no matter the type of company or colleagues you work with.

Additionally, I will emphasize the importance of continuous learning and staying up-to-date in your field of expertise. We will dive deep into the significance of interpersonal relationships and how they are fundamental to any successful career. You will also learn to refine your communication skills and overcome the fear of failure—a barrier we all face at some point.

As you progress through the book, you will discover solid strategies for requesting promotions, becoming an effective leader, and successfully managing teams. But we won't just focus on practical skills; we'll also discuss emotional intelligence and resilience, critical factors for managing stress, overcoming obstacles, and continuing to grow in your career.

This book will not only equip you with professional tools but also help you develop the confidence to face challenges and become an authentic leader. My aim is to provide you with a guide that not only covers the technical aspects but also the human skills that will lead you to long-term success.

Get ready to absorb knowledge, develop skills, and face the challenges of the work world with confidence and determination. This is the beginning of a new chapter in your professional life. Let's embark on this journey toward success together!

AUTHOR'S INTRODUCTION AND WORK EXPERIENCE

The author of this book, at the time of writing, was working in a mid-level management position at a prestigious and highly sought-after company. He is a family man and husband striving for a better future for his family and a legacy for his son. With a career in the financial sector, he navigates the corporate world, balancing vision and idealism, while having bravely and determinedly charted a path through a sometimes-uncertain professional landscape.

Over the course of more than 20 years in his career, the author has experienced successes, mistakes, and challenges, including moments of shyness and gaps in some strategic knowledge. Nevertheless, he has risen from the lowest level to mid-management positions. His professional journey began in the early 2000s when he was a young man with dreams of prosperity and a strong determination to achieve success. Over time, he has developed a toolbox filled with strategies and practical advice that have allowed him not only to survive in the competitive corporate world but also to thrive in it.

By combining technical skills with effective management of his emotional intelligence, the author has overcome obstacles and gained a deep understanding of organizational dynamics. He has climbed the corporate ladder and seen the fruits of his work and dedication.

Today, the author shares his knowledge and experiences in this book with the purpose of empowering young professionals and those who seek to advance in their careers. His goal is to provide them with the tools needed to succeed in the competitive corporate world and to achieve their professional goals.

Now, it's time for you to write your own story in the professional world, taking advantage of the lessons and inspiration that this book has to offer.

PART I: STARTING IN THE WORK WORLD

Chapter 1: Entering the organization

The power of first impressions

In our school days, many of us enjoyed the smell of new books and notebooks before writing a single word in them. Although this experience has changed in the digital age, the first day at a company remains similar: exciting, filled with expectations, and the beginning of a new professional journey. Whether it marks the start of a long or short phase in the organization, that first day is a moment that stays in our memories. The first impression you make will be crucial as it leaves a lasting impact on how your colleagues, bosses, and other collaborators perceive you. This is a unique opportunity to stand out and establish a solid foundation for your future in the company. So, what should you keep in mind to make a good first impression from the moment you step into the company?

I. Dress code: Clothing has always been a powerful tool for making a good impression. Historically, public figures such as first ladies have used their style to project elegance, confidence, and inclusiveness, adapting to each situation. Similarly, in the work environment, how you present yourself visually influences the perception others have of you.

The image you project is fundamental for making a good first impression as a professional. Before your first day, research the company's dress code by consulting someone from Human Resources. If you're given a uniform, you won't have much to worry about. Otherwise, carefully select your outfit in advance, ensuring that it aligns with the work environment you're entering.

For example, if you're going to work in an office that requires formal attire, you can look up appropriate outfit combinations online. If possible, buy the clothes ahead of time and make sure they are in good condition and ready to wear. It's better to be slightly overdressed than to risk appearing sloppy.

I remember a time when, uncertain about the dress code at my new job, I opted for a formal suit. When I arrived, I realized I was more formal than necessary, but this helped create a positive first impression.

II. Punctuality: Some time ago, I read about a top executive from a well-known Japanese car company who arrived several minutes early for an important business meeting. Despite his high rank, he patiently waited for everyone to be present before starting. This gesture demonstrated deep respect for others' time and set a clear standard for punctuality and professionalism. The lesson from this experience is that being punctual means arriving neither too early nor late but precisely at the agreed-upon time.

Punctuality is crucial both for first impressions and your long-term performance. Arriving on time shows respect for others and establishes a standard of professionalism that can positively influence how your colleagues perceive you. For your first day at work, arriving a few minutes early demonstrates commitment and seriousness. Plan your time well, calculate how long your commute will take, and make sure you are ready to start promptly. This shows that you value your new position and take your responsibilities seriously.

III. Positive attitude and enthusiasm: Imagine Pedro, who landed a new job at a mid-sized tech company. From day one, he showed a lack of interest: he arrived late, without enthusiasm, and low on energy. He constantly complained about the tasks assigned to him and showed little interest in learning or collaborating with his colleagues. His attitude not only affected his performance but also created a tense atmosphere in the office. Over time, Pedro fell behind in the organizational structure, and his poor performance was noticed by management, eventually leading to his dismissal. It was a hard lesson. To avoid a situation like Pedro's, it's important to start your first day of work with enthusiasm and a positive attitude. Show gratitude for the opportunity and arrive with energy. Greet your new colleagues with a smile, introduce yourself cordially, and demonstrate an eagerness to learn and collaborate. Positive energy is contagious and will help you build valuable relationships from the start.

IV. Listen and learn: The ability to learn is a skill you must cultivate from your first day to your last, as humans never stop learning. The day you think you know everything is the day you've made a mistake because your ego will limit your capacity to continue growing and improving. I remember hearing a businessman say, "I'm so good that I don't need to learn anymore." Although he was successful in many aspects, his lack of humility and openness to suggestions hindered his ability to grow. The lesson is clear: there's always something new to learn.

From your first day, you will be exposed to a lot of new information. Listen attentively during inductions, presentations, and meetings. Take every word seriously, ask relevant questions, and show a genuine desire to learn. This will reflect your commitment to understanding the company culture and processes, helping you integrate effectively.

V. Professional introduction: Before your first day, prepare a brief presentation about yourself. This introduction, which you can use in future meetings, will be like a verbal business card where you include your background, skills, and professional goals. Practice this introduction and listen to it carefully, putting yourself in the shoes of those who will hear it. Being able to clearly and concisely express who you are and what you can bring to the table is a valuable skill in any work environment.

VI. Show gratitude: In an episode of a show called "Undercover Boss", a boss went undercover as a new employee at a Friday's location. During this experience, he appreciated the energy, warmth, and empathy of the bar manager while she trained him. This approach allowed him to discover aspects of the organization he wouldn't have known from his executive position. Showing gratitude is essential from your first day at work, regardless of the hierarchical level of the person who helps you. A simple gesture of thanks reflects respect and appreciation and will open many doors for you. Moreover, maintaining an attitude of gratitude and positive energy will not only benefit your personal growth but also contribute to a better work environment for your colleagues.

Remember, these lessons are especially important on your first day at work, but they are just the beginning of your journey. Keep these principles in mind, as the results will become apparent over time. Have a clear goal: to advance effectively in your career. Apply these principles to make a positive impression and build solid relationships in your workplace. With dedication and determination, you will be one step closer to achieving your professional goals.

Understand the corporate culture

On one occasion, a brilliant and highly capable executive who had worked at a pioneering internet search technology company took on a new challenge as CEO of another large tech corporation that was struggling to maintain its relevance in the market. However, one of her most significant mistakes was not understanding or adapting to the corporate culture of her new company.

This company had historically been known for its relaxed culture, where flexibility and remote work were highly valued. When she tried to change that culture by requiring employees to return to the office, she faced resistance. Many employees, accustomed to flexibility, became frustrated, leading to a decrease in morale and a talent exodus to other companies. This cultural shift accelerated the company's decline as it failed to meet the intended goals.

This example illustrates the importance of understanding and respecting the organizational culture when joining a new company. Adapting to the existing culture is key to successfully integrating and avoiding mistakes that could impact both your career and the company's performance.

After spending several years with the company and gaining a deep understanding of its culture and operations, you will be in a much stronger position to propose changes that could improve efficiency and generate more benefits for shareholders. Over time, your knowledge of the company will allow you to identify areas that could benefit from enhancements or innovations. It's important to approach these changes gradually and collaboratively, involving key leaders to ensure the transformations are implemented smoothly and without resistance. Proposing improvements with sensitivity to the existing culture will not only strengthen your position in the company but also allow you to bring significant long-term value.

Chapter 2: Developing technical skills

Continuous learning

Constant training, knowledge updates, and techniques to improve efficiency in your activities are key tools that will propel your path in the competitive work world. Imagine your profession as a vehicle that must travel a long journey; continuous learning is the fuel that will keep that engine running and allow you to move toward your goals. In this section, you'll explore the importance of continuous learning as a fundamental tool for your professional growth and how to make the most of it.

Now imagine being in the middle of a forest without a map or compass to guide you. How would you know which way to go? Continuous learning is that compass in your professional career. It provides the necessary direction to move forward and reach your objectives. In a work world that is constantly evolving—with rapid technological updates and advancing automation—staying up to date is essential to remain competitive. Whether in your area of expertise or any other field, this principle applies universally.

A software developer who graduated ten years ago as an expert in a specific programming language faces a completely different technological landscape today. Artificial Intelligence (AI) has entered the software development field, offering advanced capabilities in automation, machine learning, and data processing that are revolutionizing the creation of applications and systems. An example of AI is ChatGPT, which can generate contextual human-like text and responses, transforming user interaction in various contexts and applications.

If this developer does not invest in continuous learning to stay up-to-date with these emerging technologies, their career risks stagnation. They could miss the opportunity to participate in innovative projects using AI to enhance the efficiency and intelligence of applications. Besides ChatGPT, there are other AI tools and technologies, such as advanced natural language processing models and generative video tools, that are redefining software development.

A general practitioner who has been practicing for several years may have treated a wide variety of diseases and conditions. However, medicine, like many other disciplines, is constantly advancing. New procedures, therapies, and medical technologies are improving patient care and outcomes. If the doctor does not continue to update themselves through continuous education, their patients may not benefit from the latest advancements and most effective treatments. Staying informed about the latest medical research and technologies ensures not only higher-quality care but also offers patients more advanced and effective treatment options.

Continuous learning not only allows you to adapt to changes but also helps you stand out among your colleagues. Employers value professionals who show a willingness to constantly learn and improve. When you invest in your own development and acquire new skills, you become an invaluable asset to the organization.

Continuous learning is not limited to taking occasional courses or attending seminars. It is an ongoing learning cycle that involves being open to new ideas, challenging yourself, and continuously seeking opportunities for growth.

In your day-to-day work, there will always be opportunities to improve some activity. If you don't find them, worry, because they always exist, even if they are not always obvious. You should set a clear goal or identify a specific need to find the right niche for training. You may need to acquire a particular skill, and for that, it's important to focus your efforts effectively.

Once you define your areas for improvement, look for learning sources. These can include books, attending conferences, following blogs, taking courses, interacting with mentors or colleagues, and exploring online resources. The internet is a powerful tool for training in specific areas, even without paying for it. With careful and patient searching, you can find ways to update yourself. The key is to diversify your sources of knowledge.

Knowledge renewal

Imagine that a financial manager or accountant decides to take a bold step in their career and embarks on a process of continuous learning. They acquire new skills in programming, such as Python or R, master databases like SQL, and come to understand complex systems. Thanks to this training, they can now extract valuable data from their ERP system, identify hidden patterns in the company's finances, and develop predictive models that optimize cash flows.

This transformation not only increases their value within the organization but also makes them an agent of change. Today, terms like "Data Scientist" are becoming increasingly common, though a decade ago these specializations were virtually unknown. With this diverse skill set, it's possible to make more informed and strategic decisions, reduce costs, and significantly increase revenues.

After the global COVID-19 pandemic, the technology sector grew considerably due to the need for remote work and the increased use of technological tools like Microsoft Teams, among others. For a financial accountant who has traditionally worked with numbers, reports, and financial analysis, their profession is undergoing a radical transformation driven by a business environment increasingly centered around data.

In the past, data science was primarily reserved for systems engineers and statistics experts. However, today data is one of the most valuable assets of any company, and accountants and finance professionals have a unique opportunity to lead its utilization.

In the digital age, organizations rely on enterprise resource planning (ERP) systems to manage their financial operations. These systems generate enormous amounts of data, ranging from business transactions to spending trends. This is where understanding programming and databases becomes essential to make the most of this information.

Imagine again the financial manager who decides to follow a path of continuous learning, acquiring skills in programming like Python or R, mastering databases like SQL, and understanding complex systems. With this knowledge, they can begin to extract valuable data from their ERP system, identify hidden patterns in the company's finances, and develop predictive models to optimize cash flows.

This change not only increases their value to the organization but also makes them an agent of change. Today, terms like "Data Scientist" are common, but 25 years ago these specializations were virtually unknown. This set of skills allows for more informed and strategic decisions, cost reduction, and significant revenue increases.

The financial accountant or manager who has acquired data science skills becomes an essential resource for the organization. Their ability to translate financial data into valuable business information places them in a privileged position for success.

This example shows how continuous learning and acquiring

new skills, even in areas traditionally unrelated to accounting or finance, can propel your career and allow you to lead in an increasingly data-driven business world. Instead of limiting yourself to the traditional boundaries of your field, you can become a change agent. The motivation and dedication to keep learning will remain the keys to your success.

In conclusion, staying up-to-date in your field is an essential requirement. In today's world, where technology changes drastically every day, it is essential to have an open mind toward new ways of practicing your profession. Don't limit yourself to the traditional boundaries of your career; explore and apply options that may not have been part of your original training plan but could be crucial to standing out as a successful professional.

Don't get stuck in the past; embrace the future with confidence and determination. Keep alive your passion for continuous learning and adapting to the new realities of your profession. Only by doing so can you excel and achieve lasting success in your career.

PART II: INTERPERSONAL RELATIONSHIPS

Chapter 3: Connecting through communication

Effective communication

Communication, whether verbal or written, is one of the most powerful tools we possess. However, to be truly effective, we must learn to master it both personally and professionally. Many times, despite our best efforts to convey an idea, the message isn't understood as we intended. Whether you're writing an email or having a face-to-face conversation, it's essential to ensure your ideas are captured and understood correctly.

In a commercial company, a sales manager meets with his team to define quarterly goals. During the meeting, he uses clear presentations and charts to explain the objectives, breaks down the key performance indicators, and sets realistic deadlines. He also encourages open dialogue, urging team members to ask questions and share ideas. This effective communication ensures that everyone clearly understands what is expected of them, which, in turn, improves the team's motivation and productivity.

In a hospital, a patient undergoes major surgery. After the operation, the surgeon makes a brief visit to the patient but provides only a vague description of the procedure, without offering important details or answering the patient's or family's questions. This lack of clear information generates frustration and anxiety in an already stressful situation. The absence of effective communication causes unnecessary confusion, aggravating the emotional state of those involved.

In an important corporate meeting, a high-level executive presents a complex business strategy using technical jargon and confusing charts. The employees present struggle to understand the information, and although some ask questions, the executive doesn't provide sufficient clarifications. Some employees prefer not to ask further questions to avoid appearing incapable or unsure. As a result, they leave the meeting without a clear understanding of the strategy, leading to frustration and demotivation. This lack of effective communication undermines team cohesion and alignment with the company's objectives.

In each of the above examples, the difference between effective communication and ineffective communication is evident. The ability to convey ideas clearly and understandably is crucial to both success and people's well-being. When communication is effective, as in the sales meeting with clear objectives, collaboration is fostered, and motivation increases. On the other hand, when communication fails, as in the poorly explained surgery or confusing business strategy, the consequences are often frustration, confusion, and even demotivation.

These examples highlight the importance of developing and refining the skill of effective communication in all areas of life. By communicating clearly, we strengthen our relationships, avoid misunderstandings, and contribute to achieving shared goals. It's an essential skill that not only improves our personal and professional lives but also has a profound impact on the quality of our interactions and the achievement of our goals.

Effective communication is based on several fundamental principles. The ones that have yielded the best results for me throughout my career are:

a. Clarity and simplicity: Avoid using technical language or unnecessary jargon and present the information in a way that is accessible to your audience. Consider their level of knowledge on the topic you're communicating. For example, it's not the same for a law firm to discuss legal changes among colleagues as it is for a lawyer to explain those same changes to clients. The form and technique of communication should adapt to each audience.

b. Active listening: Paying full attention to the other person is a sign of genuine interest and facilitates a deeper understanding of their needs and concerns. It's very easy to get distracted or appear disinterested if you don't take your eyes off the computer or other devices while someone is talking. This type of behavior not only shows a lack of respect but also gives the impression of selfishness, which can lead to conflicts or misunderstandings with the other person.

c. Empathy: The ability to emotionally connect with other people's experiences and feelings is key to deeper understanding and providing a more compassionate response. Empathy is essential for effective communication. It's crucial to put yourself in the place of your audience or conversation partner, understanding their perspectives, emotions, and needs. This will allow you to tailor your message in a way that resonates more deeply with them.

d. Clarifications: Encourage feedback with an open mind and willingness to clarify doubts. Ensure that your listener or audience has understood the message, and always provide opportunities for questions or consultations. Feedback is a valuable tool for improving the clarity of communication and strengthening mutual understanding.

Effective communication is an essential skill in all aspects of life. Mastering good communication will enable you to create a favorable environment for advancing within the organization. We should never underestimate or neglect refining this skill, as its mastery is fundamental to professional growth and success. Therefore, I encourage you to develop and continually cultivate this ability.

Building strong relationships in the workplace

A few years ago, I joined a family-owned company where most of the team had prior experience in the same department. Over time, I noticed that the person in charge of the department had previously been a colleague at the same level as the rest of the team. This person was organized and ethical, but they were dismissed by upper management after an unintentional error: they failed to properly manage a tax requirement that the regulatory entity had notified, resulting in a significant fine for the company.

Upon further investigation, I discovered that there had been a form of "sabotage" by one of their subordinates. This person not only avoided reminding the boss about the requirement but also suggested waiting for further communications from the tax authority before taking action, which worsened the situation. Eventually, this subordinate was also dismissed, as it was proven that they were involved in the incident, and even worse, they lost all their retirement benefits. This is a clear example of how unethical behavior can create a toxic work environment.

The above example highlights the importance of building strong relationships in the workplace. When people get along, they are more likely to support each other and work together toward common goals. In contrast, conflicting relationships tend to create a negative work environment that can affect both productivity and overall well-being.

To build strong relationships in the workplace, it's important to keep the following points in mind:

* Be respectful and kind to everyone, regardless of their hierarchical position.

* Actively listen to others and show that you care about what they have to say.

* Maintain honesty and transparency in all your interactions.

* Be a good team player and always be willing to collaborate.

* Maintain a positive and optimistic attitude in the face of

challenges.

* Appreciate the experience and lessons you learn every day in your organization.

You can conduct a self-evaluation based on the points mentioned to see if you are applying them in your day-to-day activities. By following these principles, you will contribute to a more positive and productive work environment where everyone has the opportunity to thrive. Additionally, you will strengthen your profile within the organization by building strong relationships with your colleagues.

At the beginning of my professional life, I looked for a vacancy in a mid-sized service company for a position related to my career. The hiring manager informed me that there were no openings in my field, but there was an opportunity in the administrative area. My main responsibility was to make copies of files, documents, and writings for different departments. Although the work was simple, it allowed me to learn a lot about how the company operated. One of the things I enjoyed doing was reading the non-confidential documents while copying them, which helped me better understand their content and learn how they were structured.

On several occasions, while reviewing the documents, I noticed spelling or grammatical errors, and I pointed them out to the person who had assigned the document to me, always making sure my corrections were accurate. Most of the time, they were, and as a result, the documents were corrected and rewritten. Over time, my direct supervisor began to value my initiative and contribution to the organization, which led to me being recommended to the Human Resources Department when a vacancy opened up for a higher position.

In less than three months, I was promoted to an administrative position with double the salary. And in less than two years, I was promoted to deputy head of the department where I had started, thanks to my focus on exceeding my responsibilities and helping my colleagues identify potential errors to ensure that their reports or outcomes were flawless.

This example, based on my own experience, demonstrates how building strong relationships through proactivity at work can open up opportunities for professional growth while also earning appreciation and respect from others. It was also key to be respectful and empathetic. By following these recommendations, I was able to establish strong relationships with my colleagues and earn the appreciation of the company's leaders. These relationships helped me prove my value and advance in my career.

Chapter 4: Relationship with superiors

Strategies to earn the trust of your superiors

Earning the trust of your superiors and other leaders within the organization is essential for your professional development. This trust opens doors to new opportunities such as promotions or career advancement, improves communication, and ensures support during difficult situations. Additionally, it provides you with greater autonomy and recognition. Building this trust will help you solidify a strong professional reputation, foster a positive work environment, and expand your network and influence. All of this is key to developing leadership skills and achieving long-term success.

Below, I detail the strategies you can use to earn your superiors' trust and have an effective professional relationship with them:

a. Understand their expectations and priorities: The first step to earning your superiors' trust is understanding what they value and what they expect. Take the time to learn about their goals and challenges so you can align your efforts with what directly contributes to their objectives.

For example, Maria, a new member of a technology company's sales department, notices that her boss, Carlos, is highly focused on improving team efficiency to meet quarterly targets. In several meetings, Carlos mentions the importance of optimizing processes and increasing productivity.

To better understand Carlos' expectations, Maria requests a one-on-one meeting with him. During the conversation, she listens carefully and asks about the department's specific challenges and what he expects from the team. Carlos explains that one of the biggest challenges is managing time and resources when preparing proposals for potential clients, which often delays the sales process.

Armed with this information, Maria, who has experience with automation tools, suggests implementing software that can automate part of the proposal creation process. She develops a detailed plan showing how this solution could save time and allow the team to handle more potential clients. When she presents the proposal to Carlos, he is impressed with her initiative and the clarity of her plan.

The implementation of the tool proposed by Maria significantly improves the efficiency of the sales process. Now, the team can generate personalized proposals much faster, allowing them to spend more time following up and closing sales. Carlos, satisfied with the results, publicly acknowledges Maria's effort and initiative, highlighting her ability to understand and act on her superiors' priorities.

This example shows how understanding a superior's expectations and priorities can guide an employee to take actions that benefit not only their professional development but also the goals of the team and the company.

b. Effective and regular communication: It is essential to keep your bosses informed about the progress of your projects in a clear and concise manner. Effective and regular communication can make a significant difference. Don't wait for formal meetings; use emails or brief check-ins to keep them updated on your progress and any challenges you may be facing.

In a medical office, Ana, an administrator, is in charge of implementing a new patient management system to improve efficiency and service quality. Her boss, Dr. Lopez, is keen that the transition to the new system goes smoothly without affecting patient care.

Understanding the importance of keeping Dr. Lopez informed, Ana establishes a regular communication plan. Every week, she sends an email detailing the project's progress, the challenges encountered, and the proposed solutions. Additionally, she organizes bi-weekly meetings to discuss the implementation in person and receive direct feedback.

Ana ensures that her communications are clear and concise. In her emails, she uses bullet points to highlight key points and charts to show progress. In the meetings, she comes prepared with a clear agenda, focusing on the issues most important to Dr. Lopez, such as the impact on patient flow and staff training.

Based on Dr. Lopez's feedback, Ana quickly adjusts the project's approach. For example, when Dr. Lopez expresses concern about the staff adapting to the new system, Ana organizes additional training sessions and sets up a support system to address the team's questions.

Thanks to Ana's regular and effective communication, Dr. Lopez is always aware of the project's progress and can make informed decisions. This facilitates a successful transition to the new system with minimal disruption to patient care. Dr. Lopez praises Ana for her excellent project management and her ability to maintain smooth communication.

This example demonstrates how crucial effective and regular communication is. Keeping your superiors informed through clear updates and well-focused meetings not only aids decision-making but also contributes to project success and strengthens your reputation, opening new opportunities in the future.

c. *Take initiative:* Don't limit yourself to your daily tasks. Look for opportunities to take on additional responsibilities or propose solutions to existing problems. This shows your commitment and your ability to contribute beyond your role, always making sure that the tasks are within your reach to avoid potential overloads or mistakes. Proposing concise solutions to problems your superior or the organization faces, even when not directly assigned to you, is an excellent way to earn prestige in the eyes of your bosses.

Jorge works in the Human Resources department of a large manufacturing company. Although his primary responsibility is managing payroll, he notices that the recruitment and selection process is inefficient and causes delays in hiring essential employees.

Jorge decides to take the initiative to solve this problem. He conducts thorough research on best recruitment practices and applicant tracking software. He then prepares a detailed proposal that includes a cost-benefit analysis and suggests a demonstration of several systems that could streamline the process.

Jorge schedules a meeting with his boss, the HR director, to present his proposal. In the meeting, he focuses on explaining how the implementation of his idea could significantly reduce recruitment times and improve the quality of candidates, benefiting the entire company.

Aware of his limitations, Jorge clarifies that his intention is to present the idea and suggest that a specialized team be formed to implement and monitor it. He recommends that personnel with recruitment experience lead the project but offers to assist with the transition and training, given his familiarity with the proposal.

The HR director is impressed with Jorge's initiative and the quality of his research. He values Jorge's proactivity and ability to present a well-founded solution without being directly assigned the task. A team is formed to evaluate and eventually implement the proposal, with Jorge included as a key member due to his initiative and in-depth knowledge of the project.

This example illustrates how taking initiative, especially in areas outside of your usual responsibilities, can demonstrate your commitment and ability to contribute value to the company. By proposing well-founded solutions to problems, without overstepping your capabilities, you can significantly enhance your prestige and visibility in the eyes of your superiors, opening the door to future growth opportunities.

d. Prioritize quality in your work: Don't just focus on meeting deadlines, but also on ensuring thorough quality that minimizes the need for corrections. This advice goes beyond simply completing a task—it involves making sure every detail is carefully considered and executed. Pay special attention to the details, anticipate potential problems, and ensure that all parts of the work are well integrated. Adopting this approach will distinguish you as a professional committed to excellence, solidifying your reputation and trustworthiness in the work environment.

Luis is a financial analyst at a prestigious consulting firm and is tasked with developing a detailed financial report for an important client that will be presented at an upcoming meeting with investors.

Instead of merely compiling the financial data and presenting it in a standard format, Luis prioritizes the quality of the report. He ensures that he not only understands the numbers in depth but also the context of the client's business and the investors' expectations.

Luis delves into every detail of the report. In addition to the usual financial analysis, he includes insights on market trends and future projections. He also anticipates questions that investors might ask, such as the sustainability of the client's growth or risk management and prepares sections that proactively address these concerns.

Before delivering the report, Luis thoroughly reviews it to ensure there are no errors and that all information is presented logically and coherently. He also asks an experienced colleague to review it for a fresh perspective, ensuring that all important aspects are covered.

The report is received with praise from both the firm's leadership and the client. The quality of Luis's work is so high that no corrections are needed. The report serves as a solid foundation for the investor meeting, and the client is particularly impressed by the anticipation of questions and the depth of the analysis.

This example shows how prioritizing quality and paying attention to details can lead to outstanding results and professional recognition. By focusing on all aspects of the report and anticipating the client's needs, Luis not only completed his task but also added significant value. This improved his reputation and solidified his position as a top-tier financial analyst within the company, making him an ideal candidate for future promotion if he maintains this level of consistency in his work.

e. Learning from feedback: Learning from feedback is closely tied to emotional intelligence, which we will explore in depth in a later chapter. You should never feel uncomfortable if someone offers you advice or points out areas of improvement in your work. As Leonardo da Vinci once said, "While I thought that I was learning how to live, I have been learning how to die." This means that we are always in a state of learning. Feedback from others helps us broaden our perspective, become more aware of our areas for improvement, and deliver better results by correcting our mistakes.

Consider the case of Roberto, a project manager at a design firm. Although Roberto is known for his technical skills and creativity, he also has a reputation for not handling criticism well. During the presentation of an important project, his team receives constructive feedback from a key client, suggesting several changes to the design to better align with the project's vision.

Roberto, confident in his expertise and convinced that his original approach is the right one, immediately dismisses the client's suggestions, arguing that they would compromise the artistic intent of the project. He insists that his vision must prevail, minimizing the importance of the client's feedback and disregarding the input from his team.

This attitude creates tension within the team, which feels frustrated about not being heard and worried about the impact on the relationship with the client. Additionally, the client interprets Roberto's resistance to feedback as a lack of professionalism and flexibility, jeopardizing the long-term relationship with the firm.

Roberto's refusal to accept feedback and adapt his approach results in a final product that, although technically impressive, fails to meet the client's expectations. This damages both client satisfaction and the firm's reputation. Furthermore, the incident negatively affects team morale and the perception of Roberto as a leader. Instead of earning respect for his firmness, he is seen as inflexible and difficult to work with.

This example highlights how refusing to accept recommendations or being closed to suggestions can have negative consequences—not only for the project outcome but also for team dynamics, client relationships, and long-term career growth. Embracing and learning from feedback is essential for personal and professional development, allowing individuals to adapt and thrive in a constantly evolving work environment.

f. Dealing with difficult personalities: At work, we interact with people who, due to their experiences, have developed personalities different from our own. While we may sometimes find similarities, we will never be exactly the same. In the workplace, you will encounter various colleagues and bosses—some with challenging personalities, and others with whom you might form friendships. These interactions can be difficult to navigate, and knowing how to manage them properly is key to maintaining a positive and productive work environment. Empathy is fundamental in every interaction because it allows you to understand the other person's perspective, express your ideas clearly, and manage your reactions in stressful situations.

When dealing with difficult bosses, it is important to avoid becoming a target for attacks that can affect the workplace atmosphere and limit your professional growth. If the strategies you apply are not effective, considering a job change might be the best option to protect your emotional well-being and give yourself the opportunity to start fresh in a healthier environment.

Types of difficult bosses and how to handle them:

> Aggressive bosses: These are dominant and often irrational individuals who tend to overreact to minor mistakes and criticize publicly. Stay calm and avoid open confrontations, especially in public settings. Be assertive, back up your points with solid arguments, and find the right moments to discuss any concerns.

> Passive-aggressive bosses: These bosses avoid direct communication, resort to sarcasm, delay important decisions, and do not acknowledge the efforts of others. Encourage direct communication, set clear expectations, and agree on specific responsibilities and deadlines to avoid misunderstandings.

> Narcissistic bosses: These individuals constantly seek attention, take credit for others' work, minimize others' contributions, and lack empathy. Protect your self-esteem and present your ideas in ways that also support your boss's goals, which may help you earn their favor and minimize conflict.

In general, it's essential to maintain an empathetic and strategic attitude, ensuring that conflicts aren't perceived as personal attacks. Communicate your ideas in a way that benefits both your area of responsibility and your boss's, reinforcing their self-esteem. Remember the advice of Sun Tzu in *The Art of War*: "Keep your friends close and your enemies closer."

Professionalism and ethics as a subordinate

Being a good subordinate isn't limited to completing the tasks assigned to you; it also involves adopting practices of professionalism and ethics that strengthen the relationship with your superiors and promote a positive work environment. Below are some key points for being an effective team member:

Avoid criticizing others

Criticizing coworkers or even superiors not only affects team cohesion but can also damage how your bosses perceive you. Negative comments foster an atmosphere of distrust and negativity, which can harm both the team and the organization.

Ana works in the marketing department and has some disagreements with her colleague Juan, who is responsible for social media. Instead of discussing the issues directly with Juan to resolve their differences, Ana constantly complains about him to other coworkers, even to her boss. This behavior not only affects team morale but also causes her boss to question Ana's professionalism, wondering if she might speak poorly of him in other circumstances, creating an atmosphere of distrust.

Criticizing others can lead your superiors to lose trust in you. If your boss perceives that you are more focused on criticizing your coworkers than on solving problems or adding value, they may question your loyalty and commitment to the team. Moreover, this behavior can generate unnecessary conflicts and contribute to a toxic work environment.

Instead of criticizing, focus on problem-solving and maintaining open, respectful communication. If you have a conflict with a colleague, seek a direct and professional resolution. When speaking with your superiors, concentrate on the work and how to improve team performance, avoiding negative remarks about others.

Key phrase: *"If you speak poorly of others, you'll likely speak poorly of me too."*

Avoid constant complaining

Constantly complaining about assigned tasks or the work environment can give the impression that you're not committed to your job or that you don't appreciate your position in the company. This attitude can be interpreted by superiors as a lack of motivation or even as a sign that you don't want to continue working for the organization.

Carlos, a financial analyst, frequently complains about the workload and tasks assigned to him. Although he fulfills his responsibilities, his constant complaints raise concerns with his boss. Hearing Carlos' complaints makes his boss wonder if he really wants to stay with the company or if he's just waiting for the first opportunity to leave.

Constant complaints can make your boss assume that you're unhappy in your job and perhaps looking for an exit. This can affect your growth opportunities within the company, as your superiors may hesitate to assign you important projects or recommend you for promotion.

Instead of complaining, look for constructive ways to express your concerns. If you feel that certain tasks are overwhelming or believe you could contribute more in other areas, request a meeting with your boss to discuss how to optimize your work or take on new responsibilities. A positive and proactive approach will show that you are committed to your role and focused on solutions rather than problems.

Key phrase: *"If I spend my time complaining about my activities, it will seem like I don't want to work here."*

<u>Propose solutions instead of just presenting problems</u>

One of the most valued traits by superiors is the ability of a subordinate to not only identify problems but also propose viable solutions. Simply bringing problems to your boss without having considered possible solutions can make you seem like someone who avoids taking responsibility or lacks the initiative required for your role.

Laura, a project coordinator, notices that one of the regular suppliers is delaying deliveries, which is affecting the project's schedule. Instead of simply informing her boss about the problem, Laura researches alternatives and presents a plan to either change suppliers or renegotiate terms with the current one. Her boss appreciates Laura's proactivity and values her ability to address the problem with practical solutions, which reinforces his trust in her.

If you constantly present problems to your boss without suggesting solutions, you may be perceived as someone who is not fully committed to the organization or who lacks the skills needed to tackle challenges. This can negatively impact your reputation and limit your growth opportunities.

Before presenting a problem to your boss, take time to analyze the situation and think of possible solutions. Even if you don't have the perfect solution, showing that you've thought about the problem and are actively looking for alternatives will demonstrate your commitment and professionalism. Additionally, this will relieve some of your boss's burden and strengthen the trust in your relationship.

Key phrase: *"If you only bring problems and expect your boss to solve them, you're not acting professionally or fully in your role."*

In summary, adopting practices of professionalism and ethics as a subordinate, such as avoiding negative comments about others, steering clear of constant complaints, and proposing solutions rather than just pointing out problems, is essential to maintaining a positive relationship with your superiors and ensuring a productive and harmonious work environment. These practices not only reflect your integrity and commitment but also position you as a valuable and trustworthy member of the organization.

PART III: MOVING UP THE CORPORATE LADDER

Chapter 5: Asking for promotions and advancements

Don't directly ask for promotions or advancements

Do not directly ask for promotions or advancements. While this advice may seem counterintuitive, it's actually more effective to let your performance and preparation speak for themselves. Instead of explicitly requesting a promotion, use a more subtle strategy: let your work and accomplishments position you as the ideal candidate for new opportunities. If you follow the principles and advice outlined in the previous chapters, you will naturally stand out without having to ask for it.

The key lies in consistency and excellence in your day-to-day performance. If you meet and exceed the expectations of your current role, your superiors will notice your value. This indirect approach also avoids giving the impression that you're only seeking a promotion for personal ambition, demonstrating that you're genuinely prepared to take on greater responsibilities.

It's essential to maintain a proactive attitude and show your willingness to take on new challenges. This means that even if you don't directly ask for a promotion, you're always ready to take the initiative in important projects and demonstrate that you can handle additional responsibilities. Over time, this behavior will be recognized, and when a promotion opportunity arises, you'll be considered without needing to explicitly request it.

In a multinational company operating in several countries, a significant restructuring took place in the administrative departments of one country. These departments were divided into three business lines, each with its own hierarchical structure and legal entity, although all belonged to the same corporate group. Each business line had around 10 employees, totaling 30 across the country.

The restructuring merged the three business lines into a centralized structure. Of the original 30 employees, only 13 were retained: those who demonstrated exceptional performance and strong commitment to the company's goals. The others were informed that their contracts would not be renewed.

Among the retained employees was a supervisor who had been a key figure in their business line. This supervisor was known for their consistent and high-quality performance. Additionally, they stood out for their proactive attitude, problem-solving skills, and willingness to take on new challenges. Their reputation preceded them not only among colleagues but also at the higher levels of the organization.

Despite the drastic changes, this supervisor never asked for a promotion. Instead, they let their work speak for itself. Every project they led, every problem they solved, and every innovative idea they proposed reinforced their image as a natural leader within the company.

Senior management, recognizing their value and the positive impact they had made on the organization, decided that this supervisor was the right person to lead the new centralized structure. Without needing to ask for it, they were promoted to head of the administrative department as a recognition of their dedication and skills. This promotion was not only the result of their excellent performance but also of their ability to adapt and excel in a constantly changing environment.

This example demonstrates that by following the principles of consistent performance and proactivity, you can be considered for promotions and advancements without needing to explicitly ask for them. The key is to continuously demonstrate that you're prepared to take on greater responsibilities, letting your actions speak for you instead of making explicit requests.

Identify opportunities

Knowing how to identify opportunities within your organization is an essential skill for career advancement. Imagine an employee who sees a vacancy in an area they're interested in. Instead of immediately applying, they first decide to consult with their boss. This dialogue is important because it shows respect for the hierarchical structure and a desire to gain perspective before taking action.

In this case, the employee meets with their boss to discuss their interest in the vacancy. They explain that they've seen the opportunity and would like to know if their boss considers them a good candidate. This type of conversation not only opens the door to valuable feedback but also shows the boss that the employee is interested in growing within the company and values their opinion.

By taking this initiative, the employee gains a clear understanding of their strengths and areas for improvement, which allows them to prepare better. Additionally, this type of communication strengthens the relationship with their boss and makes them aware of the employee's aspirations, which could result in support for future opportunities.

Let your preparations be known

Preparation is key to success, and it's important that your superiors are aware of the efforts you're making to improve your skills.

In casual conversations, you can mention the courses or certifications you're completing. For example, in an informal chat with your boss, you might mention a recent course and how the skills you've acquired can benefit the team or the company. This type of interaction not only shows your commitment to professional development but also your interest in contributing to the success of the team.

By sharing your progress naturally, you keep your boss informed of your development without it seeming like you're seeking recognition or a promotion. Over time, as your boss sees how effectively you apply your new skills, you'll be in a better position to be considered for a promotion without having to directly request it.

These indirect approaches to advancing in your career are effective because they allow your actions and results to speak for themselves. By focusing on your development, identifying opportunities, and naturally sharing your achievements, you position yourself as an ideal candidate for promotions and advancements without having to explicitly ask for them. This not only protects your reputation but also allows you to grow steadily and solidly in your profession.

Chapter 6: Becoming a leader

Don't miss opportunities

Don't miss opportunities. If you've followed the previous topics and are still not managing a team or a person, you're very close to doing so. Accepting opportunities and challenges is key to your professional growth. In an organization, the moments when you are offered leadership responsibilities can be decisive for your career. Turning them down—whether out of fear, uncertainty, or lack of preparation—can negatively impact how your superiors perceive you and, consequently, influence your future within the company.

Accepting challenges, even when you feel insecure, shows your willingness to grow and learn. To your superiors, this attitude is a sign that you are ready to advance within the organization. On the other hand, a negative response may be seen as a lack of ambition or confidence in your own abilities.

Imagine you're in the process of being hired by an organization, and during the interviews, they ask if you would be willing to lead an important project to implement a new system. Even though you feel you lack experience in project management, you accept the challenge and request training in that area to meet the expectations. This response not only demonstrates your willingness to take on responsibilities but also shows your honesty and desire to continuously improve.

For the organization's leaders, your willingness to take on new challenges is a signal of your growth potential. Rejecting a challenge can raise doubts about your ability to face bigger problems in the future, which could limit your opportunities for advancement. Therefore, whenever you're offered an opportunity, take a deep breath and accept the challenge. If you feel you lack knowledge, be honest and request the necessary training. This proactive attitude strengthens your image as someone willing to learn and guarantees success in every task.

A friend who worked for a multinational company shared his experience when he was offered a significant opportunity at work. He was responsible for coordinating warehouse activities, ensuring that inventories were always up to date to guarantee product availability. One day, his superiors proposed a huge challenge: managing the supply chain logistics in all the countries in South America where the company operated. He knew this was a unique opportunity to grow professionally, and when he asked for advice, I suggested he accept the challenge. I told him that taking on a challenge of that magnitude would not only make him stand out but also demonstrate his desire to grow within the company.

A year later, we met again, and I was surprised to learn that he had been fired. The official reason was that he didn't align with the company's values, but what really shocked me was his confession.

He hadn't accepted the challenge to manage regional logistics because he prioritized his family life. He explained that he wanted to see his daughters grow up and that taking on that responsibility would have meant spending weeks or even months away from them. I realized that while professional growth is important, it shouldn't always be the priority. This friend taught me a valuable lesson about the importance of maintaining a balance between personal and professional life. Family, friends, and even physical and mental health are key factors to consider when making career decisions.

This experience left me with an important lesson: success is not always measured by the amount of responsibility we take on or the promotions we achieve. Sometimes, true success lies in making decisions that allow us to maintain a healthy balance in our lives, prioritizing what really matters.

Developing leadership skills

Leadership is not a gift one is born with; it is a skill that is developed and perfected over time. Several authors have written about the competencies that make an effective leader. Among them, Stephen Covey, in his book *"The 7 Habits of Highly Effective People"*, teaches us how certain key habits can transform both personal and professional lives. There's also John C. Maxwell, who in *"The 21 Irrefutable Laws of Leadership"*, describes universal principles that every leader must follow to influence and guide effectively. And Daniel Goleman, in his work on *"Emotional Intelligence"*, explains how managing both one's own emotions and those of others is essential to leadership. These references are fundamental, but now I'd like to share what has personally worked for me throughout my career:

A. Clear communication: A good leader must be able to convey an idea precisely and understandably. It's not enough to speak; you must ensure that the message is received as intended. The key lies in using the right words, a firm but empathetic tone, and, most importantly, in verifying that the message was understood. How to achieve this? Always ask if what you've explained has been understood, and if possible, ask your team to summarize what they've grasped. This gives you the opportunity to correct any misunderstandings before they become a problem.

B. Emotional intelligence: While this concept will be covered more in-depth in Chapter 7, it's crucial to note that without emotional intelligence, a leader can quickly lose connection with their team. The ability to manage your own emotions and understand others' emotions is critical for success in any leadership role.

C. Decision-making under pressure: Decisions made under pressure are often the most visible and decisive. Leaders cannot afford to hesitate when time is limited. However, this doesn't mean acting without thinking. A good leader is transparent when more information is needed to make a decision, but they also know how to manage timelines so that responses are timely. Imagine that during a production crisis, you have to decide whether to stop the production line or continue under risk. A good leader would quickly evaluate the risks, ask for additional data if necessary, and make a decision that maintains the team's confidence in their leadership.

D. Self-criticism: No one is perfect, and a leader must be their own toughest critic. At the end of each day, take a few minutes to reflect on your decisions, conversations, and actions. Ask yourself: Did I do the best I could in that situation? Could I have handled that conflict better? This exercise will help you improve constantly. Many professional speakers review recordings of their presentations to identify areas for improvement. You can apply the same principle to your leadership: take note of the important decisions you make and review how you could refine them.

E. Mentors and role models: One of the most effective ways to learn leadership is by observing those who already do it well. It's not just about admiring public figures but identifying leaders close to you whom you can observe in day-to-day life. Often, a casual conversation with a more experienced leader can offer valuable lessons that books don't teach. If you could share a meal or an informal meeting with a senior leader, seize the occasion to ask about how they handled difficult situations or what advice they have for improving leadership skills.

Leading teams effectively

An effective leader knows they cannot treat all their team members the same way in every situation. The key to successfully leading a team lies in adaptability and the ability to understand that each situation requires a different approach. Sometimes, it's essential to be understanding and empathetic, while other times, it's necessary to take a firm stance and demand appropriate performance. Finding this balance can be the difference between a productive team and a dysfunctional one.

Adapting leadership to circumstances: Not every workday is the same, and not every situation requires the same response. A good leader knows when to be flexible, recognizing that team members have human needs like family or study leave, and granting that flexibility builds trust and loyalty within the team. However, it's also important to know when to set clear boundaries and make tough decisions if necessary. For example, one of my team members was logging many overtime hours, but a colleague pointed out that they might be abusing the flexibility. After reviewing the system and security cameras, we discovered that although the employee had logged a document at 7 p.m., they had left to meet friends and returned around 1 a.m. to log another document to justify overtime hours. The evidence was clear, and I decided not to approve those hours. The employee claimed they needed the money for their family expenses, but we handled the situation professionally based on the facts. Despite this intervention, months later, we had to terminate the employee as their personal problems and lack of control affected their performance.

Empathy and professionalism: Being an effective leader doesn't mean always being lenient. It's essential to correct team members when necessary but do so respectfully and professionally without compromising trust. Empathy is key to understanding the difficulties each person faces, remembering that we all go through stages of growth and personal challenges. However, this doesn't mean tolerating behaviors that affect productivity or the team's ethics.

Fostering a trusting environment: A leader must create an environment where team members feel comfortable speaking openly, even about delicate topics such as seeking new job opportunities. A trusting environment allows employees to express their concerns without fear of retaliation. This type of open communication makes it easier to make fair and equitable decisions, maintaining the team's integrity.

Recognizing the team's strengths and weaknesses: A good leader knows how to identify the skills and attitudes of their team members. Not everyone has the same abilities, and it's important to assign responsibilities based on individual capacities, preventing some from taking advantage of the leader's empathy. This discernment helps prevent conflicts within the team and maintains a fair and balanced work environment.

Leading effectively means being adaptable, acting with empathy and professionalism, fostering a trusting environment, and using good judgment to manage situations that may affect team dynamics. It's not about being lenient all the time but about knowing when and how to exercise authority fairly and transparently.

PART IV: FINAL ADVICE FOR PROFESSIONAL SUCCESS

Chapter 7: Developing emotional intelligence

Definition of emotional intelligence

Emotional intelligence, a concept popularized by psychologist Daniel Goleman, refers to the ability to recognize, understand, and manage both our own emotions and those of others. Unlike intelligence quotient (IQ), which measures cognitive abilities, emotional intelligence focuses on how we manage our emotional responses in everyday situations, particularly in the workplace.

From an evolutionary point of view, our brain has developed in layers. At the center lies the amygdala, part of the limbic system, which regulates our most primitive emotional responses, such as fear, anger, and aggression. This brain structure was crucial for our ancestors' survival, enabling them to react immediately to threats. However, in the modern work environment, acting impulsively can be counterproductive. This is where the prefrontal cortex comes into play, regulating rational thought and decision-making. This part of the brain allows us to assess situations consciously, plan, and regulate our emotions before acting.

Numerous studies have shown that when the amygdala becomes highly activated, it can hijack the functions of the prefrontal cortex, leading to what is known as an "emotional hijacking". This phenomenon explains why we sometimes act impulsively and regret our actions later. In the workplace, these reactions can damage professional relationships, reduce productivity, and affect decision-making.

A study conducted by TalentSmart found that 90% of top-performing employees have high emotional intelligence, indicating that the ability to manage one's own emotions and those of others is a critical indicator of professional success. Furthermore, research from Yale University has shown that work teams that foster emotional intelligence exhibit greater cohesion, fewer conflicts, and better collective decision-making.

The importance of emotional self-regulation

Emotional self-regulation is an essential skill in any professional environment because it allows individuals to control their emotions, especially in high-pressure or conflict situations. It's not just about managing our own emotions but also about avoiding being provoked by others, whether intentionally or not, who may try to destabilize us emotionally. Staying calm in the face of these challenges is a sign of emotional maturity and professionalism.

In many cases, conflicts within a team can escalate quickly if emotions are not managed properly. This is particularly critical in leadership teams where impulsive decisions or personal confrontations can have significant consequences for the organization. Self-regulation doesn't mean suppressing emotions but managing them consciously, avoiding impulsive reactions that could damage relationships with colleagues and harm one's professional image.

In a meeting of the executive team of a large multinational company, two senior managers were discussing a recent project that had failed to meet its objectives. One of the managers, Juan, publicly blamed Pedro, another manager at the same level, for an error made by one of Pedro's subordinates. Juan criticized Pedro's lack of control and supervision, which, according to him, contributed to the project's failure. Although the initial comment was professional, it quickly took on an accusatory and personal tone.

Pedro, feeling attacked, began to experience an intense emotional reaction. His amygdala, the part of the brain responsible for managing emotional responses, triggered a "fight or flight" response. Instead of processing the criticism rationally, Pedro started raising his voice, interrupting Juan, defending his team, and taking the criticisms as a personal attack. As the conflict escalated, Pedro lost his composure and was on the verge of physically confronting Juan.

In this case, Juan's provocation, although unintentional in provoking such an extreme reaction, employed a psychological tactic that exacerbated the situation: public criticism. By calling out Pedro in front of other senior executives, he touched Pedro's ego, making him feel vulnerable and embarrassed. This triggered a negative emotional response that Pedro failed to control. His lack of self-regulation nearly led to a physical confrontation, which would have had serious consequences for both him and the reputation of the executive team.

In the best-case scenario, Pedro could have maintained his calm upon hearing Juan's criticism, taking a deep breath before responding. Instead of interrupting, he could have let Juan finish speaking, showing a calm and professional demeanor. Then, in a measured and respectful tone, Pedro could have thanked Juan for his comment and acknowledged the area for improvement, focusing on solutions to ensure the issue didn't happen again in the future. By remaining calm and objective, Pedro could have de-escalated the situation and demonstrated leadership, earning respect from his colleagues.

Managing stress and work pressures

Work-related stress is a reality that we all face at some point in our careers, and knowing how to manage it is essential for maintaining our mental and physical health. I remember when I was responsible for leading a project to overhaul the entire IT system of a multimillion-dollar company. Although I tried to stay calm and focus, the problems and delays with the project deeply affected me. I started experiencing involuntary eye twitches, neck pain, and difficulty sleeping. This kind of stress accumulated over weeks and manifested physically, signaling that something was wrong.

One of the best decisions I made to manage that pressure was to take a vacation. Disconnecting completely from work for a few days allowed me to recharge and return with a fresh perspective. I've also recommended to colleagues that when they feel overwhelmed, they should prioritize their well-being above any project. Work can continue, but our health and quality of life should not be put at risk. A couple of days off or a vacation can be crucial in helping you return to your responsibilities with greater clarity and energy.

A study published in the Harvard Business Review found that employees who take regular breaks and use their vacation time have higher productivity levels and fewer symptoms of burnout. Companies like Google and Salesforce have implemented wellness policies that include relaxation spaces and stress management programs to preserve their employees' mental health and reduce the effects of burnout. These initiatives reflect a growing understanding that productivity isn't just about the number of hours worked but also about quality of life.

Throughout my career, I learned that when stress is not properly managed, it can have serious consequences. After nearly 14 years working for a company where I eventually led the administrative side of 34 national businesses, the stress and lack of time for my family led me to make a difficult decision: to resign. I spent my days in endless meetings, answering emails late into the night, and receiving calls from my superiors even on weekends. Not only was I not being compensated financially for the increasing responsibility, but my health and well-being were at stake. I decided to take a leap of faith and look for a new company that would offer me not only better financial benefits but also a better quality of life. In less than six months, I found a company that provided challenges but also the balance I needed.

It's important to understand that our career should not compromise our health or personal life. While work can be a source of satisfaction and achievement, we must know when to pause and take care of ourselves. Recognizing the signs of stress and taking steps to alleviate it—such as proper rest, exercise, and temporary disconnection—can make a significant difference in our long-term well-being.

The most valuable lesson I want to share is that sacrificing your health or family life for an excessive workload is not worth it. Sometimes, the best decision is to step back, reevaluate your priorities, and find an environment where you can grow professionally without compromising your quality of life. The key to advancing successfully in your career is finding that balance between professional effort and personal well-being.

Developing emotional resilience

Since I was young, the idea of being called out for a mistake has always made me extremely uncomfortable, and I've never liked that feeling. For many of us, facing correction or criticism can be tough, and what usually happens is that we react with a mix of frustration and embarrassment. I've experienced this many times. However, what initially seems like a flaw can also be an opportunity to develop an essential skill: emotional resilience.

Resilience is not simply "toughing it out" in the face of adversity; it's the ability to adapt, recover, and move forward after making mistakes. Personally, when I make a mistake, I tend to dwell on it for days, analyzing every detail, wondering what I could have done better, and what decisions led me to fail. This self-criticism can become so intense that it interferes with my performance, affecting my confidence. Over time, I've realized that the energy I invest in lamenting what I didn't do well could be better spent growing and learning from the experience.

It's important to emphasize that making mistakes is part of

working life, and it shouldn't permanently affect your self-esteem. The challenge lies in breaking the cycle of negative thoughts and replacing them with actions that push you forward. I've had to learn myself that not every mistake deserves days of reflection; sometimes, the best thing we can do is accept that we are human and not infallible.

When we start to see mistakes as opportunities, emotional stress decreases. At first, it may seem difficult, but the key lies in practicing resilience. If we look at it with perspective, every failure we face has something valuable to teach us. Learning to handle criticism and our own mistakes is not easy, but in doing so, we strengthen ourselves emotionally, and that has a huge impact on our professional careers.

To anyone reading this, I'd like to say that the path to resilience is not something achieved overnight. It's a continuous process, a habit that develops over time. We can't control every situation we find ourselves in, but we can control how we respond to them. And in that response lies our emotional strength.

CONCLUSION

Throughout this book, we have explored how to climb the corporate ladder, based on the experiences that have proven effective for me. From the importance of first impressions and continuous learning, interpersonal relationships, emotional intelligence, and leadership, all these tools are essential for achieving professional success. The key is to apply this knowledge consistently and strategically.

The path to success is not easy, but it's not impossible either. There are many ways to reach it, and some may even be better than the ones I've detailed in this book. My goal has been to provide you not only with the tools that have worked for me, but also with the confidence that every step you take will be valuable. No matter what stage of your career you're in, every day is a new opportunity to grow. Difficulties are inevitable, but your ability to overcome them is what will make you stand out. You have the power to shape your professional destiny, and this book is just the beginning.

A Chinese proverb says, "The best time to plant a tree was 20 years ago. The second-best time is now." This message applies not only to those just starting in the workforce, but also to those who have been in it for years. It's never too late to act, learn, and evolve. So, whether you are at the beginning, middle, or end of your career, there is always room to reinvent yourself, enjoy life, and take care of yourself, your family, and friends.

The fear of failure is one of the biggest obstacles in our careers. Self-doubt is normal, but what's important is not letting those doubts paralyze you. Mistakes are a natural part of the process and offer valuable lessons. With resilience, you'll learn to see failure not as a roadblock but as a steppingstone to success. The key is to keep trying because true failure lies in never trying at all.

www.ingramcontent.com/pod-product-compliance
Lightning Source LLC
Chambersburg PA
CBHW070949220526
45471CB00007B/2958